The Great

Exorcism

*The Influence of Demons and Devils
across Centuries of Spiritual Tradition*

By Arthur Crane

PANTIANOS
CLASSICS

Published by Pantianos Classics

ISBN-13: 978-1-78987-303-0

First published in 1915

Contents

Preface

In 1904, I published my first book, "The New Philosophy" and I gave away more than 29,000 copies, refusing to take payment for a single one.

I then explained that I did not need money, that I had a sufficient income to provide for my needs and pay for the book as well, that it was my delight to give the book free — that other men spent money on what pleased them, and I was merely spending money on what pleased me. Further, I said that I would not sell the inspiration of the truth that had come to me — that truth had no price; but I also said I would not put myself in a position to be called mercenary. Others, who were teaching, praying and healing, but who themselves were not free from want, were charging so much per folio for their inspirations, and the world had its little joke at their expense, for, "the practice of truth," said the world, "should not be mercenary." But I was, and still am, and please God, ever shall be, free from want, yet I was then too lately emancipated to know that I could have handled the whole world's coin without fear, favor, or one instant's thought of danger of criticism.

In 1908, I first published my second book, "All Mysteries," of which I gave away no copies whatever, but about 4000 copies have been sold.

This is a book of action, not contemplation. Herein I show that an humble instrument of the CHRISTPOWER without merit in himself, can nevertheless act that POWER in you.

This is a living faith. It has life now, independent of the past. It has joy now, independent of the future. But the principal thing it has is POWER.

To such as cannot or will not grasp the point of view, or trust the CHRISTPOWER, this book will nevertheless be of interest; for it makes the most sweeping claims, and, whether one is able to accept it or not, it is certainly offered in perfect sincerity and humility, as an inspiration of the highest character.

Though I am personally a Counsel of the Supreme Court of the United States, and the recipient of other honors, I count nothing that this world can give as of the slightest value in comparison to the POWER herein explained. So I want no title. Call me neither "Honorable," "Esquire" or even "Mr."; just, plain —

Brother Crane.

Chapter One - The Origin of Evil

What was the origin of evil? Materialists would give one answer, students of mythology a second and theologians a third:

(a) The Materialists answer would be that originally there was nothing, except atoms of matter at a distance from each other absolutely still and absolutely cold. There were no governing principles or natural laws, only a tendency to exist. Age followed age and a hardly perceptible movement began among some of the atoms. This was the beginning of consolidation and temperature, which from the materialists point of view was an improvement. So the first "tendency to exist" now became divided into two tendencies, **the tendency to exist unimproved, and the tendency to improve.**

These two tendencies or wills have been opposing each other ever since and were born into all nature. Man, they say, developed by steps and stages from the earliest combination of atoms, opposed at every stage by that portion of the universe, (or by that tendency to exist unimproved at all times animating toward him that portion of the universe), less advanced than himself. Thus the tendency to exist unimproved manifests itself, by animating in lower life a hatred for the higher, and materialists have a theory that material germs, or low forms of life, flying through the air and entering the body of man, cause all diseases. Again, whether it be poison of the body or of the mind, it is this tendency, fighting man in the one case by lower forms of matter, in the other by suggestions of lower life. Sin, they say, is yielding to the spirit of unimprovement.

When at last man was born he became conscious of the struggle between these two tendencies, and alternately falling into the power of the one, and being inspired by the pure idealism of the other, he has progressed, it is true, but stumblingly and haltingly, with the horde of tendencies just behind him, always more and more powerful to pull him back into the abyss. Every stage of development left behind represents a separate tendency doing its best to draw us back to that stage. So as man progressed more and more he had more and more tendencies (the materialists' devils) to contend with.

The logical conclusion would be that the IDEAL is man's guardian angel and beastliness his devil. But we can not expect people calling themselves materialists to use other than material terms.

(b) Students of mythology give a hundred fanciful personal names to the tendencies of both kinds. One kind were "gods" and the other kind demons or dragons. Both kinds were given offerings, the gods in order that they would befriend in time of need, and the dragons so that they would not devour the whole of the people. The offering to the dragon was very usually a

maiden, sometimes chained to a rock like Andromeda. It may be that the form of the dragon was suggested by some survival of pterodactyl or dinosaurus, but in any event it was the ancient type, the power of a past stage of development. On the other hand the "gods" were ideals. They were personifications of qualities, such as wisdom, swiftness, power, beauty, etc. Here again we have the eternal struggle between the bestial and the ideal, between the tendency of the dragon to exist and the tendency of man to rise.

These gods were not all powerful nor were they the authors of evil. They usually caused good to come out of evil, but that was only in the sense of "making the best of a bad job." Progress as represented by the mythological gods, made good come out of evil by using evil as a brake, so that all phases of development should keep pace with each other and not one outrun the "team." "Forward, but not too fast," seems to have been its motto. The separate power of evil was known and recognized and no one denied its existence.

No one does now, as far as I know, except in a way, viz., some tell us to combat evil by denying its existence. The ordinary layman naturally replies, "If it has no existence why combat it?" This answer does not feaze them in the least; we are told to combat the seeming existence of evil by denying its reality. By its reality is meant its power to effectively prevent the advance, progress and development of man. And the student of mythology would hold this to be true as to the race and type but not as to the individual. The gods, it was said, were powerless to save the royal line of Croesus to the throne of Media, nor could they help any individual after his fate, howsoever accidentally, had been pronounced. They did save Andromeda from the dragon, but that was a special dispensation, and besides, her fate had not been pronounced by the "Pythoness" or evil spirit of the Delphic oracle.

It would seem then that only a very unselfish man could ignore the existence of evil, which as far as he personally is concerned, is a threat of real and irreparable disaster, but he has the unselfish satisfaction of knowing, that if such disaster should come upon him, or Ms loved ones, out of that disaster, the spirit of progress will cause no harm to come to the race as a whole. I may fearlessly walk this earth, scorning accident, disease, misfortune, sorrow, pain, slander or death, if my mind is set only on the advancement, development, and progress of mankind as a whole. This, in a rational being, with a calculating, analyzing brain and a warm heart, could not be, unless he felt such a kinship to mankind as to be an indivisible part of the whole, inseparably allied to what he felt to be the one spirit of advancing life, and destined to live on, in that spirit, to and through what glorious development the future ages may have in store, regardless of what happens to his body, his individuality, his achievements or his loved ones. This is the height of unselfishness reached by those who sincerely deny the reality of evil.

(c) Theologians say that in the beginning was the Logos, i. e., the Word, the Ideal, the Advancing One. There were in heaven, also, vast numbers of angels. These angels became divided into two bands and fought a mighty battle in heaven when the band headed by the rebellious angel Lucifer was defeated and cast out of heaven. However, the rebel angels, now called devils, landed safely on the Earth, to which the struggle has been transferred, and is now taking place in the heart of man. The demons of our age were angels of a bygone age. They once were loyal to the Word, but failing to keep up with their loyalty it became necessary to declare war upon them, which war has been continued ever since. Every man hears "the voice of Jesus calling" on the one hand and is "tempted by the devil" on the other. Sometimes the devil assumes the form of an angel of light and deceives man. God, say the theologians, cannot prevent man from being deceived and tempted by the devil, but he can punish those who fall. The theologians are divided in their opinion as to the physical reality of eternal torture in Hell. A prominent preacher, Pastor Russell, does not believe in a hell at all, while others preach all the horrors of the "lake of fire which burneth forever and ever, where their worm dieth not and their fire is not quenched." It may be that the idea of eternal and everlasting punishment came first in contemplation of the serpent, which, as an animal, seems to be fixed, and incapable of developing into anything higher. For it to lose the capacity for development is an

irrevocable sentence to stay as it is for eternity; it is a loss of birthright, never recoverable. If the devil be the "tendency to exist unimproved," then such a fate is literally falling into the clutches of the devil for ever and ever.

Other races of vegetable and animal life seem to be "fixed." These are the races that have died the death eternal. The lizards and "missing links" of the past, now extinct, have not died in this worst sense because they have died but to live again in advanced forms. To become "fixed" would therefore be the worst death for a race.

By the theologians, again, we are told to imitate the example of One who counted his own life as nothing that the race of man might be saved. A new ideal to which we shall press forward, though the individual may be despised, rejected and slain. Thus, and only thus, they say, can we overcome in that terrific conflict still being waged between the forces of good and evil. Here again no thinking man can be ready to sacrifice all for that Divine Ideal unless he feels a Oneness with the race, a vital gladness in the thought of its advancement and a consciousness that his real ego is identical with the imperishable Logos.

Here, then we have three distinct histories of the origin of evil, but the difference between them, from an analytical point of view is more a matter of names and of personifications than of substance. Men have just as gladly laid down their lives to fight the evils seen by science, and to fight the dragons imagined by mythology, as they have for the sake of the ideals of religion. As far as the individuals were concerned, they went down, but who shall say that one single one of those deaths was in vain, for the advancement of the race and the glory of those ideals for which they died?

No one can escape the conflict with evil. No one can be sure that he will not suffer and die in that conflict. The most one can do is to forever refuse to surrender.

The theory of the constant advancement of the race being the Good tendency or power, involves the necessity for the simultaneous and spontaneous birth, in every being born, of an Ideal.

The Ideal, thus incarnated, seems an imperishable picture, or image, of an advancement not yet realized.

This Ideal is the soul. Now, if a race should be born without that Ideal, all progress would cease and the race become "fixed," because century after century might pass and still the race, without the Ideal, could not advance, for the Ideal is the only spark of advancement, and without it the race would fall forever into the power of the Tendency to exist unimproved.

This brings us to the proposition, that one animated by soul will never find his or her ideal man or woman. For the Ideal implanted in the breast is not for the purpose of comparison with the race as it now is, but for the purpose of being born in the flesh, and to be realized in the next, or in future, generations.

Theologians tell us that man is the only animal endowed with Soul or Ideal. Man is the only animal now advancing — and all other animals are "fixed," not possessing that eternal spark of the Logos or Ideal.

Those who cannot see that there are any evil powers, or that there could be any power except the "all-powerful good," find it difficult to explain the accidents, horrors and calamities which befall even the "righteous."

That "good" is all-powerful, in the way the word "omnipotent" was first used, may be admitted; namely, that it is a stronger power than evil, and will win in the end. But the thoughtful man will not of himself evolve a theory blaming every accident or other adverse event upon the "good" power, nor will he of himself think that such are "visitations of the wrath of God," or are sent to us by the Divine will because they are "good for us." It obviously would not be necessary, to an omnipotent power, to destroy a city by fire, or sink a boat-load of innocent excursionists, in order to teach to the bereaved the doctrine of patience. Neither would He do evil that good might come if He were omnipotent good. Again, by the standard of right and wrong implanted in the human breast, it would not be possible for the Ideal Good to have wrath, or to destroy our lives to appease it; and Bible students tell us that the Hebrew word translated "wrath," should more properly have been translated merely as a synonym for power.

Neither would it be possible that the Divine Good should be the author of what mental aberration in ourselves or kinks in our environment, are translated by the words "sin, sickness and death."

Although these things are not real in the sense that they will not conquer in the end, to those who suffer humiliation through sin, as well as to those who feel the "claims" of sickness and those who are bereaved by the "claims" of death, these things are very real, as real as anything that comes to their consciousness. Whether the cause of them be the evil influence of the tendency or will to exist unimproved, or the evil influence of demons or devils, the result is the same. The opposing WILL, adverse to mankind, is the power ever laying its hands upon us in hate and attempting to draw us back into everlasting death. That adverse will, although less powerful in the end than the will of the Ideal or CHRISTPOWER is still a belligerent, and. must be recognized as such, whether we personify it under various names according to its various aspects or not. The battle ground is everywhere. Each one knows the phase of the great adversary most pressing against him. To the materialists, no less than to the idealists, the battle is a real one. The difference is one largely of names and personifications.

Should we then fold our hands because we believe good will triumph over evil in the end?

Can we supinely surrender to the evil powers now, in the knowledge that in any event the human race will not be injured by our cowardice, because the Power of Good is able to bring good out of evil?

Those are the questions which each one has to honestly face in his own heart and much depends, for him, on the answer that he gives.

Man's body is the temple of the living Logos or Word. Man's soul, the only I am, is that Logos. In any event the "I am" within us will overcome evil in the end, but because the battle with the evil powers threatens that sense, which we have, of individual or separate life, we must not individually or separately surrender, or even rest quietly under the attacks of the enemy.

Chapter Two - The Secret Power

Materialists hold that matter in small particles is all that exists, and that by a peculiar arrangement these small particles "organize" into flesh and blood. They do not believe in "influences," good or bad. They do not believe that Christ "cast out" devils, or now can; and yet they believe that these infinitely small invisible particles, called electrons, *know where to go,* and by the force of their own knowledge and will, form themselves into atoms also so small as to be invisible, of various different substances. They say "nothing exists but electrons." Then, they say, those atoms of various substances, combine in various proportions to make "molecules" and that thousands of molecules make a simple cell, and that such cells form muscle, blood and brain. None of them have ever seen, in the strongest microscope, an electron, an atom, a molecule, or such a cell. But because they consider some material theory necessary, they say those invisible things make up the universe.

As to the question of how thought may be produced, the scientists were formerly divided. Many owned they were puzzled on this point, but they now all agree that those invisible entities which they call electrons are able, in some mysterious way, to segregate themselves; then, seeming to know where to go, these electrons form combinations in our bodies which produce thought, will, idealism and even love.

An invisible entity that knows where to go, and produces thought by its combinations in our bodies, is the present belief of materialists, and is the modern successor of the ancient belief that "a million devils could dance on the point of a needle."

Materialists admit that sometimes these electrons, or ions, start going the wrong way, bringing all kinds of trouble. Their problem then is how to get rid of them. They say that if a finer, stronger, electrical force could be brought to bear, the electrons which had determined to go the wrong way, could be driven out of the system, curing all ills, mental and physical.

A little thought, and we will discover that these are precisely the same impressions as others receive, but under different names.

Let the scientists conceive of those influences which they feel, as invisible "ions," running riot of their own perverted will, within them. They are then in exactly the same helpless fix as if they conceived them to be "demons" — until that superior POWER is invoked which can conquer.

In other words, it makes no difference, either in the suffering, or the remedy, whether they name the INFLUENCES "ions," or "demons," or what they name the POWER that saves them.

All peoples, nations, churches and schools, are converging toward a common understanding of the INFLU-

ENCES that affect the lives of men. Whether they are called electrons, ions, manias, demons, or spirits, there is a common knowledge of their inferior power, and a common instinct that somewhere there is a SUPERIOR POWER which can cast them out.

"Influences," we will see, are living, invisible beings. In all races their power has early been felt, and they are now recognized universally under various names, such as "obsessions," "guides," "spirit forces," "Elementals," "Earth spirits," and under other names and disguises, as explained elsewhere.

Man has always been in slavery to these "influences," and it will be well to consider not only the universal experience of mankind in ages past but also the present feeling in every tribe and nation of primitive people, where such feeling seems to have come spontaneously and identically to far separated nations, indicating that there is something, whatever we may call it — some influence, which those peoples actually feel.

So it was from the earliest dawn of history. Influences have always been felt. Even before the ancient Aryan migration the primitive people of the East called them "demons."

"In the beginning there was," saith an ancient writing, "but one man, and there came to tempt him, one demon. Men died, but demons did not die, and each generation was oppressed, not only by its own demons, but by those of the generations which went before." [1]

Allatu was the name given the Queen of Hell by the Babylonians, and Namtar was the name given the plague demon who brought sickness and disease. Their secret names were engraved on certain tablets of destiny, which, it was believed, would thereafter come into the possession of ONE who would have power over Allatu and Namtar, by virtue of the knowledge of that secret name, and of the secret name of Ra or God. Tiamet was another name for the Queen of Demons, who was also the foster mother of the terrible influences which stultify the brain. Tiamet was identical with "Behemoth" and with "Ishtar the Daughter of Sin," who came to men in dreams to tempt them. She was also identical with Astarte.

Shutu, the demon of tempest and war, was identical with Abaddon.

The struggle of man against influences is the whole history of the world. Every religion has been an organized effort to "cast out devils"; every war has been a temporary ascendency of INFLUENCES; every progress has been accompanied by progressive INFLUENCES, so that "Evil" can be said to have progressed no less than civilization.

The Buddists in India sought to combat the evil INFLUENCES which oppressed their lives. These INFLUENCES were then called "Asuras." It is said that these ancient influences are still dwelling with us, invisible, malevolent and powerful. Also that many other and younger spirits afflict mankind and now threaten to destroy us utterly.

But for the CHRISTPOWER, it would be terrible to know of the awful unseen influences; such knowledge would drive the strongest unaided human brain insane, and unless the reader is willing to be put to the choice of insanity or acceptance of the CHRISTPOWER, he should read no further. Knowledge of the truth without acceptance makes the mind peculiarly susceptible to influences. They fasten themselves gradually upon you, bring dreams and imaginings, seem to set the rest of the world against you, and torment you into insanity and death.

It is not "truth" which will have these awful consequences, but your deliberate neglect to accept the CHRISTPOWER. Better harden your heart, seek not to advance and develop, than delve for curiosity's sake, and expose your mind to these forces without the armor of the CHRISTPOWER.

The ancient Persians recognized the oppressions of INFLUENCES, and separated them into classes, calling the most oppressive one "Ahriman," and the twenty-eight next worst, "devs." Ahriman then created an infinite number of evil spirits and made an egg containing "the force of spirits of the darkness." All these forces or "influences" slip into the body, according to the belief, and produce all diseases; and into the mind and produce all malice. It was declared that ultimately One would arise, having power over all those spirits, devs and influences;, and free mankind.

That these beliefs all arose from the consciousness of such INFLUENCES;, there can be no doubt, and it is equally certain that every such influence still exists — as much alive to-day as ever — and subject only to the exercise of CHRISTPOWER — to which alone it must bow.

In the ancient Egyptian system the name given to the chief influence was "Set." Here again there were a host of spirits, each one powerful over man in some particular direction, and destined to torture him until the day should dawn when the "Master spirit should arise, put down all other spirits and free mankind from their power."

In ancient Greece, according to Empedocles, the influence of a host of malevolent demons was felt, each one of a different grade, but all destined to plague man, from which plague it was supposed, no relief could be obtained.

Alexandrian philosophers gathered from every known country the experiences of man, and combined all the systems or tables of Earth spirits in one. In this table were classified thirteen kinds of demons.

First, False gods, whose Prince is Beelzebub.

Second, Slandering spirits, whose head is Apollyon.

Third, inventors of mischief and creators of anger, whose Prince is Belial.

Fourth, malicious revenging devils, whose Prince is Asmodeus.

Fifth, devils which blind men to the truth of their manhood, whose Prince is Satan.

Sixth, devils who corrupt the air and cause plagues and diseases, whose Prince is Meresin.

Seventh, the destroyer, causing wars, tumults, misunderstandings, uproars, etc., whose name is Abaddon.

Eighth, the accusing, calumniating devils that drive men to despair, whose Prince is Diabolis.

Ninth, the devils who tempt men to hoard gold, and love it, holding before them a false vision of more gold, leading them ever into want and failure, whose King is Mammon.

Tenth, Moloch, Prince of tears, pressing down on men all sorrows and disappointments.

Eleventh, devils who work injustice, whose Prince is Lucifer.

Twelfth, spirits who cause the best intentioned plans to fail, the demons of "bad luck," whose Prince is Antichrist.

Thirteenth, spirits who deaden the intellect and perception, who make man speechless when he should speak or make him speak foolishly when he would have better kept quiet; their Queen is Astarte — she also comes in dreams, with her legion of incubi and succubi.

It may be from these thirteen kinds of INFLUENCES, bringing thirteen kinds of evils, that the number "13" first was known as "unlucky."

However, it is sure that all those kinds of INFLU-ENCES still exist, though we no longer call them "dev-ils." Let us deny, if we can, that Beezlebub, Apollyon, Be-lial, Asmodeus, Satan, Meresin, Abaddon, Diabolis, Mammon, Moloch, Lucifer, Antichrist and Astarte are the right names of those living invisible influences that enslave and torture man to-day; yet no man on looking within, on his own tortured soul, or without, on the in-justice and disappointments of the world, can deny that these influences are as much ALIVE to-day as they ever were — that they are strong in the high places of the earth — and that the fulness of time is at hand, when the CHRISTPOWER exercised humbly by ITS servant — when that power — and in all humility I say it — SHALL cast them out!

These names of the thirteen powers of evil always had a measure of psychic power, but besides these names, there were secret names for each. Each secret name, if uttered, brought on immediate corresponding disaster. Even now a curious mental effect is produced by the mere utterance of the ordinary names of the thir-teen "powers."

The secret names should only be pronounced by one through whom the CHRISTPOWER is exercised, for the purpose of casting out those dreadful INFLUENCES.

One of those secret names was revealed to Jacob Boehm, and to him was given a very large measure; of the CHRISTPOWER; but he declared "that he could not, without peril to his soul, disclose the secret name of Lucifer, so tremendous would be the consequences."

Many writers have gathered data of the INFLUENCES felt in the so-called dark ages. Of the books so compiled, one of the most instructive is "La Sorciere," by J. Michelet, a copy of which is still to be found at the Congressional Library at Washington. According to all those writers the pervading demons were those who entered into women and transformed them into witches. Michelet quotes forty other authors all to the same effect.

Every time great hate was caused by great oppression and this great hate mingled, in the soul of a woman with her natural great love, a new devil was felt to be born in her.

"Who says the old devils are dead?" asks Michelet. "They must be still alive. Where are they? In the desert, on the moor, in the forest? Ay; but above all in the house." People felt themselves to be double, felt that *other* within them, became wasted and weakened more and more, and the weaker grew their wretched bodies, the more they were worried by the devils. In women, especially, these tyrants dwell.

And not ourselves only, but all nature, alas! becomes demoniac. If there is a devil in a flower, how much more in the gloomy forest! That divine morning Star, whose glorious beams not seldom lightened a Socrates, an Archimedes, a Plato, what is it now become? A devil, the arch fiend Lucifer. In the eventime again, it is the devil Venus who draws me into temptation by her light so soft and mild.

Again, when feudal powers were forming, there was here and there an independent soul who tilled his own land and held it, not under another man, but as a freeholder. He was the especial mark of spirits. His land would bear nothing, spirits swept it clean by nights. There was felt the hoggish spirit of Satan. Men were made serfs, without hope of resisting despair — and so the hate was distilled, that, mingled with the love of fireside, begat the little devils in the world that now have grown big, and storm and rage. And because women bore the hardest terrors of that terrible time, so it was mostly in women's souls that those little devils were born.

In France they were called goblins, in Switzerland trolls and in Germany Kobolds or nixies. The woman says at first, "What matters? He is so small," and Michelet adds this significant question, "Should we too feel reassured, we who CAN SEE more CLEARLY?

The INFLUENCE of Satan arose out of an overwhelming despair, under the weight of dreadful outrages and dreadful sufferings. Before the will could be reduced to the dreadful pass of selling itself to Satan forever, it must be made thoroughly desperate. It was needed the pressure of the age of iron, of cruel deeds; it was needful that hell itself should seem a shelter, an asylum, by contrast with the hell on earth. In the year 1300, the feudal lord first demanded payment in gold, the INFLUENCE of the demon Mammon gaining ascendency in that year. The world was changed. All were desperate, then the little fireside demon of Satan whispers to the woman's heart that God has forsaken her, that earth is hell, that she should give herself to him, and he will help her against the world. This is the origin of Witchcraft, a madness so universal in the dark ages that even in our own time some remnants remained over, down from those middle centuries.

Michelet gives the name Leviathan to the leading demon of trickery and evil speaking. He adds that in the 16th century there were 6500 Leviathan devils in a girl named Madeline, used by certain persecutors to give false evidence against those accused of witchcraft.

In Webster's work on the subject, [2] a case is given, with every appearance of authentication, of a child who accidentally overheard an exorcist pronounce the secret name of Abaddon, one of the so-called Princes of evil. The child afterwards repeated the word over and over till such lightnings were induced from the sky that the whole village was, like Sodom, destroyed.

There was known to be a hidden name of God, which would be revealed to whom He chose in due season. That One was to come, who, by virtue of that Hidden name, would know the secret names of every kind of demon. Solomon was supposed to possess a signet ring with that hidden name of God engraved upon it, which gave him command of the spirits. The Jewish historian, Josephus, assures us that God taught Solomon the secret names by which demons were to be expelled and diseases healed. But the Name was lost for a time till Christ came, and the CHRISTPOWER. Not by any personal merit can the revelation of that Name be obtained. It is a Name of power, and is revealed only in order that, in the fulness of time, it should have that effect which should be the WILL OF GOD.

A review of history shows that the madness now afflicting the world is only one of a sequence of general obsessions.

One madness was lycanthropia, which began about 1200 A. D., and spread until toward the end of the sixteenth century. Oppressed by this "madness of satan," men believed they were wolves, day work was demoralized and the population could be found prowling around at night, howling and fighting. This obsession spread through the whole of central and southern Europe, but by the year 1598 a reaction began; men who had "recovered" persecuted those who were still "mad," thousands were put to death; one judge alone, in the district of the Jura, put 600 lycanthropes to death.

During the same period a strange dancing madness broke out. On July 1, 1374, the whole population around Aix-la-Chapelle rushed into the city and began to dance. They danced in circles with the utmost violence, till at last they sank to the ground, groaning fearfully. According to the historians, the victim seemed to see spirits of the air. and called out the secret name of the demon Meresin; all who heard that original name immediately became afflicted with the same disorder, and danced, as if by compulsion, till they, in their turn fell down exhausted, and called out, in their turn, that they had seen the awful spirit whose secret name they announced, thus bringing still others into the snare. In that way the disease spread in a few months over the north of Europe. Those who came, incredulous, to witness the phenomenon, were themselves seized, the moment they heard the secret name of Meresin, with an irresistible impulse to dance, and they became dreadfully ecstatic in their turn. It was literally the "dance of death," and swept the country like a scourge, till, two centuries later, the secret name of Meresin was said to have lost its power for a season, and no more victims were fascinated by the contagion.

Persecution followed, as usual, and. one would think, the INFLUENCE inspiring the persecution was no less a demon than that bewitching the dancers. One class of the people were afflicted with what we may call the Meresin INFLUENCE and the other with the Asmodeus INFLUENCE — causing stern, cruel, avenging persecution of those who are deemed to be *"possessed"*; but the avengers were themselves possessed no less than the others, though differently. Asmodeus is assuredly as bad as Meresin!

In our own time, by the ripening of forces, or by the development of secret powers, the world is given over to the triplet madnesses of war, disease, and lucre. The influences, called of old by the names of Abaddon, Meresin and Mammon, have more seeming power in this day and age than ever before.

Whole nations are in love with war. They have a great passion for war itself. None know what they are lighting for — nor seem to care — the INFLUENCE which eggs them on does not reveal his name. If a soldier, spurred on, as he believes, with the holy fire of love for his flag, should be told that he was under an undesirable influence, whose name in ancient days was called Abaddon, he could not believe it, because that influence lures its victims by a vision of military "glory," so bright that it shuts out all else.

There is also a madness of disease oppressing mankind, the like of which has never appeared before. The individual who is really free from pains and aches is an exception. Classified as fevers, colds, nerve pains, liver complaints or what not, even the daily salutation has become, "How are you?" and the answer, "Quite well, thank you," shows that it is generally thought necessary to deny the existence of pain and sickness.

Many people believe themselves to be well, who have become so accustomed to the Meresin INFLUENCE that they can stand it without complaining. Patience has been learned by them to such an extent that they can now be patient under their bodily troubles as a matter of course. To them even one day of real freedom would be a revelation of joy.

It is the fashion among the comparatively well to pretend to perfect health. Others, even while suffering, reason that since there is a God causing omnipresent good, no evil can be real; ergo, the suffering must be an obsession of the mind. This obsession, or spirit, oppressing them, they claim, is very sensitive, and if its real existence be denied, it will vanish. Hence it becomes right, and necessary to them, to deny that they feel pains or aches or feel oppressed or sick. With them it is largely a matter of definition. They, too, will admit, when the right words are used, that the "claims" of disease and pain are more numerous than ever before.

Again, this day and age is one of money-madness. Nearly all are short of money; they are not in privation, but "in want." No matter how much one has he feels a want for more. Mammon dances before him with a flickering light, ever promising, never fulfilling, and those whose souls are most strongly bound to this IN-FLUENCE never get the money independence they so anxiously crave. Blind is the money-mad world, blind, blind! How foolish to think that, by spiritual slavery, physical independence can be achieved! We hear of those with wealth untold. If they really have all they want, they are the few who are free from this INFLU-ENCE. Mammon says, "Worship me, and I will make you rich," but alas for those credulous enough to believe it! Every opportunity slips from their grasp; none of their plans or dreams come true, and those that owe them money are by this INFLUENCE prevented from paying it. For this is the INFLUENCE that drives men crazy with the love of money. Cunning enough to know that if its victim gets plenty of money, he is not so likely to be en-thralled, the INFLUENCE prevents him from ever attain-ing. Like a will-o'-the-wisp, it ever leads on, never arriv-ing, pretending to invite to a feast of golden fruitage, and instead dashing its victims over a precipice of debt, disappointment and despair.

[1] Attributed, perhaps erroneously, to Hecataeus, who was ac-corded by Herodotus the honor of being the first historian.
[2] Referred to in 5 Am. Cyc. 795.

Chapter Three - Literature on Influences

Sir Walter Scott left a collection of letters on demonology and witchcraft, asserting that "the universal belief of the inhabitants of the earth in the existence of spirits is grounded on the consciousness that speaks in our bosoms."

The Celtic tribes possessed, in common with all others, a natural tendency to the worship of the evil principle — and there are many still alive who, in childhood have looked with wonder on certain patches of ground left uncultivated because, whenever a plowshare entered the soil, the Elementary spirits were supposed to testify their displeasure by storm and thunder.

R. C. Thomson, by researches in ancient parts of the world, has collected photographs of ancient clay tablets originally written in the Sumerian language of Mesopotamia. They are all invocations against INFLUENCES. Part of number IX may be translated:

Invoke the great God

That the evil spirit, the evil demon, evil ghost,

Fever and the heavy sickness which is in the body of the man,

May be removed and go forth!

O, evil spirit! O, evil demon! O, evil ghost!

O, Sickness of the heart!

O, Heartache! O, Headache! O, Toothache! O, Namtar!

Be ye cast out!

"In Egypt," says T. Witton Davies, [1] "Disease was considered due to demons, and certain formulae, when recited, drove the demons out."

Now, in every land, the belief in evil spirits is universal. Among the Chinese, Dravidians, Arabs, Singalese, etc.

In the early Church, infant baptism originated in the view that until baptism the child was in the power of an evil spirit.

In the book of Tobit of the Apocrypha, the first mention of the demon Asmodius is made under that name, and it is told that he killed seven men but that Tobias overcame him and drove him into Egypt.

Demons may now be designated according to the diseases they induce.

Among the Assyrians, demons were at first named after diseases due to them. Afterwards the name became the same for the disease and the demon.

To the innumerable company of demons belong the seven evil spirits whose names and full character are mysterious. They sow the seeds of discord in family life.

To bring about strife, quarrels and wars, is their delight. There is no disease which they may not induce. All conceivable ills they produce and promote.

Demons were also believed by the Egyptians, as by others, to bring about sickness, death and all sorts of misfortunes.

A. E. Waite has compiled a large book of the history and description of the names given in times past to the various influences. In this book, entitled "Black Magic," he gives the words of each ritual whereby the actual apparition of each spirit can be invoked, warning readers against using them by saying that "to the extent that these processes are practical — and it would be absurd to suppose that the seering processes of ancient magic did not produce seership — they are dangerous."

There can be no extensive literatures without motives proportionate to account for them. The literature referring to the INFLUENCES as demons is exceedingly large.

A great many of these works are collections of religious charms against demons.

The "Grand Grinmore" claims to be the magnum opus, the greatest book of the world — the priceless treasure, King Solomon's own writing. What other man would have had the hardihood to reveal the withering words which God makes use of to strike terror into the demons and compel them to obedience? He soared into heaven and learned the secret words of power; he penetrated the remotest haunts of demons and forced them to obey him.

The three strongest demons were Lucifer, Beezlebub and Astaroth (or Astarte). Then Lucifuge Rofocale, who was identical with Mammon and Baal and many others, all of whom as far as the influences which reached and affected man were concerned, were capable of being segregated into the same thirteen classes now recognized.

The principal exorcism was the pronunciation of the secret name, ADONAI.

In the Book of the "Sacred Magic," translated from the original Hebrew into French and thence into English by MacGregor-Mathers, [2] the names of 328 demons are given, of which 316 are divided into twelve groups, and the other twelve are superior. These names are headed with the names of Lucifer, Satan and Belial — with Leviathan (identical with Apollyon), and Astaroth, Asmodeus and Beelzebub. The original author, "Abraham the Jew," adds:

"Infinite be the Spirits which I could have here set down but I have thought fit to put only those whom I have myself experienced.

"In the name of the most Holy Adonai, the true and only God I pray and conjure you to be the declared enemy of all the evil spirits during the whole of your life.

"The rage of the demons is so great and their grief so poignant at the advancement of the human race and their own degradation, that there is no evil which they will not be ready to work, they being always attracted by the idea of the destruction of humans."

Daniel Defoe, in a very old volume which may still be seen at the British Museum, says that the demon Abaddon, first appeared to an Arabian in the Court of one of the most ancient of the Pharaohs and told him to foretell that the Ethiopians were about to attack Egypt, like a big black elephant, and advise the King to make war first in anticipation. Even to-day that INFLUENCE works in the same way by suggesting to one country that some other is about to make war on it — thus causing it to begin the war — and feel forced to do so.

M. D. Conway has written two large volumes on Demonology, which can be obtained, if not now out of print, from Holt & Co., of New York.

Every degree of ascent of the moral nature, he says, has been marked by innumerable new shadows east athwart the mind and life of man. Every new heaven of ideas is followed by a new earth, but ere this conformity of things to thoughts can take place, struggles must come and the old demons will be recalled for new service.

The demonization of diseases is not wonderful. To thoughtful minds not even science has dispelled the mystery of disease and liability to contagion. A genuine observation by primitive man is bound to suggest a connection between diseases and unseen influences.

In the legend of Harischandra, martyr to truth, the Indian prototype of Job, not the least of the martyr's trials was the attack upon him by a great horde of demons in the desert.

In the time of Paul the dark problem of the origin of evil and its continuance in the universe still threw its impenetrable shadow across the human mind. It was a terrible reality.

Rabbinical lore had repeated again and again that in the beginning, Samael (identical with Abaddon), was the fiery serpent; Lilith (identical with Astarte), the crooked serpent, and from their union were born Leviathan, Asmodeus, and all other evil INFLUENCES.

But no ancient writing gives a theory or explanation of the origin of evil. Although the Assyrians and Jews both believed that there was a revolt in heaven, we find no adequate intimation of the motive by which the rebels were actuated. The theory which Milton has made so familiar; that Lucifer aspired to take the place of Jehovah, must, however, have been popular in the time of Isaiah.

It seems that this writer agrees in the last analysis with scientists and philosophers generally.

The devils are the personifications of the will to live in any form, unadvanced, who first in heaven fought a great battle against the WILL TO LIVE IN ADVANCED

FORMS, and Were cast out to the Earth, where they oppose man — because man is capable of advancement — redemption — and eventual glorification, whereas the personification of the will to live in unadvanced form can never rise; hence the significance of the curse to the garden of Eden tempter: "On thy belly shalt thou go," forever.

The dismal conditions now between nations, he adds, (writing in the 70s), seem to have so little root in political necessity that even now one might dream that the subtle INFLUENCE comes from the red planet Mars that has approached the earth.

In Gnosticism, some explanation of the existence of evil INFLUENCES is attempted. In the beginning existed Bythos (the Depth); his first emanation and consort was Eunoia (Thought); their first daughter is Spirit, their second Wisdom. Wisdom's emanations are two — one "Ideal," the other "Material."

Here again we have the two opposing forces, the Ideal, looking toward advancement and development, and the Material, looking toward the perpetuation of unadvanced forms.

These two forces the Gnostics personified as Christ and the World. After the Material goddess had created the Earth, Wisdom, the mother of the Ideal, transferred to man a ray of that divine light.

The Material Will, finding that man had the divine spark impossible for the Material spirit to obtain, became enraged with a terrible envy and took form as a serpent, and the name of Samael. And by magical power imprisoned mankind in the dungeon of Matter, from the woes of which he can only be freed by the Ideal or Christ.

The Material will, was to Paul, "the Prince of the Power of the Air," and it is not wonderful that the ancients should have ascribed to a diabolical source the subtle deaths that struck at them from the air. The Tyndalls of a primitive time studied dust and disease, and called the winged seeds of decay and death "aerial devils," and prepared the way for Mephistopheles (devil of smells), as he in his turn for the *bacterial* demon of modern science.

A Mussulman legend says that the demon Iblis asked Allah how he should contend with man, and he was answered,

"Thy progeny shall be more numerous than his — for every man that is born there shall come into the world seven evil spirits."

The Asmodeus spirits represent the pride of life and jealousy and revenge.

The demon Mammon appeared to King Radbot in the days of St. Wolfram, and offered to lead him to a house of solid gold. The demon, disguised as a traveler, led the way to a house of gold "of incredible size and splendor."

As soon as they went in, the house vanished, and the party found itself in a dismal swamp, from which it took them three days to extricate themselves.

The INFLUENCE called Mammon, ever has lured man on and ever disappointed him.

Asmodeus, Conway goes on to say, was chained for a time by Solomon, through his knowledge of the supreme spell, or real name of God. At the time the demon was chained he had drunk some wine. Now this very demon had been the one to make wine intoxicating, for he had slaughtered in the first vineyard a sheep, a lion and a hog, with the result that the wine when drunk first gave the drinker the quality of a sheep, then that of a lion, and finally that of a hog.

Solomon in his pride afterwards boasted that he could overcome the demon even without the ring containing the secret name, and took off Asmodeus' chains for the trial. The demon instantly transported Solomon to a place four hundred miles away, to the Court of Naomah and Rahab, where he remained for a long while. Meantime Asmodeus, assuming the form of Solomon, sat on his throne.

As to the demon, Satan, this writer says:

"Beastliness is not a character of beasts; it is the arrest of man." It is not the picturesque donkey in the meadow that is ridiculous, but the donkey on two feet; not the bear of zoological gardens that is morally offensive, but the rough, who cannot always be caged. The scientists' theory of the law of evolution presents the same solution of evil as the ancients knew under the name of demonology.

The pride of the peacock, the wrath of the lion, beautiful in their appropriate forms, became, in the guise of a man uncontrolled by reason, the vices, which used to be called possession, and really are insanities.

No monster ever conjured up by imagination is more hideous than a rational being transformed to a beast.

Some scholars who listen to sweet vespers may think the conflict is over; if so, they can learn that "men are possessed of devils just as much now as they ever were."

The ethnical origin of the nightmare was the demon mare (Mara) of Scandinavia, and in ancient Ceylon we find a demoness "having the form and countenance of a mare."

E. A. Wallis Budge, in a large number of expensive illustrated volumes on Egyptology, traces the effect on that ancient race of the influences to which the Egyptians felt subject.

The spirit or spirits opposing the advancement of the human race, being the real demons, it would naturally follow that the gods of one age should seem the devils of succeeding times. Thus Hathor, worshipped by the Egyptians from the earliest dawn of history, was at first clothed with all the virtues of the patient cow, but afterwards became the queen of Hades and identified with Venus or Astarte.

The same process is seen in the serpent, which was worshipped by the Egyptians as the god of wisdom, ages before it came to be regarded as the form of the archfiend Satan.

Isis was at first a divine goddess, but afterwards became a witch or sorceress and dealt in poisons. She created a snake to bite the god Ra so that she might learn his secret name which was a word of power.

The oldest spirit known to the Egyptians was by them called Apep the storm demon, and perhaps the oldest papyrus in existence is the "Book of Overthrowing Apep." To do this, according to the papyrus, one had to recite the demon's secret names of which seventeen are given.

A princess, having been taken ill, it was felt that she was possessed of a demon; when one who knew the words of power approached for the purpose of exorcising it, the demon acknowledged its defeat in advance and promised to depart, asking as a favor that it might afterwards join at a dinner or feast, the exorcisor idealist. The demon who possessed the princess recognized in Khonsu a being who was mightier than himself, and, like a vanquished King, he wished to be on good terms with his conqueror.

William Carlisle, in a book printed in London in 1827, on "Evil Spirits," and of which there is a copy at the British Museum, recognizes all the kinds of evil influences that oppress mankind.

As scientists, by the aid of microscopes, have discovered to us vast tribes of insects which before were totally unknown to us, so Revelation discovers to us myriads of spirits — enemies more powerful "than flesh and blood."

The book is a very learned and logical work based throughout on the Bible, and showing conclusively that the demons, or spirits, or, as we would call them, IN-FLUENCES, on the one hand, and the redemption from their power, on the other, is the whole theory, plan and completeness of the salvation of, and taught in, the Holy Scriptures.

The oldest known clay tablet from the ancient ruins of Mneveh, now to be seen at the British Museum, is marked with characters which have been translated:

"I who am smitten with disease, whom the hand of the demon ..." (here the surface is broken.)

"The spectre that striketh fear, that for many days has been bound on my back and is not loosed, who attacks my face, my eyes, my back, my flesh and my whole body." [3]

A book published at the price of $25.00, entitled the Divine Mystery, by R. Swinburne Clymer, may be seen at the Congressional Library at Washington. It para-phrases a Roman Catholic promulgation by Father Sin-istrari, entitled, "Demoniality."

Elemental spirits suck the vitality of those who are weak and especially of drunkards. It has often been observed that drunk-ards' lives are the safest from accidents; this is because the Elementals take care of them, and preserve them in dangers, in order that they may continue to draw their vitality from them. When they have accomplished their purpose and drawn all the vitality out of their victims, the drunkards die, not so much from any pathological reason, as from spiritual depletion.

This is the reason it is so hard for a drunkard to reform; there is always "something" urging him to drink.

Clymer divides the spirits into four kinds: Sylphs, Gnomes, Undines and Salamanders. These Elementals derive their names from the four elements, air, earth, water, and fire. "The throne of Paralda, Queen of the Sylphs, is to the East; of Gob, Prince of the Gnomes, to the North; of Nicksa, Princess of Undines, to the West, and of Djin, King of Salamanders, to the South."

In George Rawlinson's famous notes upon Herodotus, he assures us, at page 188, that the Delphic Oracle was in reality possessed of an evil spirit, the demon of deceit, leading Croesus to make war on Cyrus on purpose to lead him to his own destruction.

[1] "Magic." Published by deLaurence-Scott Co.
[2] See Manuscript in the Bibliotheque de l'Arsenal at Paris.
[3] "Babylonian Cuneiform Texts" by Leonard W. King.

Chapter Four - False and Slandering Influences

The mortal finds himself in a world of sunshine and flowers. He finds himself conscious of his great destiny. He feels himself able, if left alone, to work out that destiny and stand on his own feet, serene and perfect.

But, though he knows that there is, or should be, a perfect system of things, wherein he has his perfect place, "something" prevents him from its attainment.

The reader may be one of those who start out on the highway of life with high hopes and exalted spirits, only to find that on every hand there exists a conspiracy against him, as it were, — a conspiracy of slandering thoughts and false estimates. With his high standard rebuffed at every turn and false standards flaunted in his face, he can no longer stand untouched and uninfluenced, but dreads what every day may bring, and every day, finds such dread more than justified.

A strong sense of justice and right is born in such an one, a gift highly desirable and supremely valuable. Yet his very gift becomes the prey of INFLUENCES, and makes the victim more susceptible to the injury brought about by these INFLUENCES, and more bitterly wronged than he could be, if he had never had that fine sense of justice and right.

The INFLUENCES make his very words appear to others as unworthy of himself and as suggesting thoughts he never would have entertained. False standards of life are brought about by the INFLUENCES formerly known as "false gods," a different INFLUENCE for each false standard. The Slandering INFLUENCES are closely allied, for they slander the sense of right by intimating that the victim has those particular false standards which he hates the most.

The reader if troubled by such influences in his life, will, upon occasion, find his friend, perhaps his dearest friend, unaccountably cold. A shadow comes between friend and friend, between brother and brother, and. even between man and wife. That dear friend, or brother, or husband, all at once seems to believe your motives are alien to him; the cloud settles down between you, and the INFLUENCE triumphs. Again, even strangers will, when this INFLUENCE is upon you, look suspiciously at you, and you feel like a pariah and outcast.

These INFLUENCES, which for convenience we may call Beelzebub and Apollyon influences, have driven many men to insanity and suicide.

Chapter Five - Influences of Malice, Anger and Revenge

Our fathers, when they felt caught in an atmosphere where anger was created spontaneously in the hearts of men, and where mischief against them seemed to be in the very air, called that obsession by the name of the demon Belial.

Similarly, when malice and revenge surrounded them, permeating the expression of their lives and mercilessly threatening the very existence of their souls, the power under which they were so victimized was called Asmodeus.

For the purposes of classification we may still call these INFLUENCES the Belial and Asmodeus influences.

That their power on earth has not diminished, everyone will agree. To some victims, it seems as though a mysterious INFLUENCE were stirring up mischief. And those suffering from the malice, or so-called "malicious animal magnetism," of the Asmodeus INFLUENCE are numerous.

These INFLUENCES cannot be conquered merely by good intentions. It is not necessary to read the personal history of every person whose history has been written, or of any one of them, to realize that the human, treading the pathway of life, with the best and most noble intentions, however conscious of his own internal honesty, always meets and is always wounded by, these almost omnipresent, though inferior powers.

For deliverance from angry and malicious INFLUENCES many have laid down their lives, and to be subject to those INFLUENCES, unless help can be obtained, is worse than death.

Anger, mischief, malice and revenge so surround man, that he, in turn, absorbs those INFLUENCES in his soul, and becomes their servant and tool. If a man's life has been thwarted by these INFLUENCES, so that at last their nature has entered into him, and he has become a medium or expression of that same malice, anger, mischief and revenge, his very soul has become tainted. Such an one is more to be pitied than blamed, — it is more his misfortune than his fault. This is the great misfortune indeed! To lose the life of your body is bad, but to lose the life of your soul is worse. By the same reasoning it would seem a greater risk, to reject the help held out to save you from this danger, than it would be to refuse to wear a pair of strong boots if you were walking in jungle-grass full of deadly snakes.

The INFLUENCES are worse than any physical snakes. Their venom is poison to your career and opportunities, as well as to your physical life and to your very soul. The air is full of currents of malice all around you, circling round and round, more poisonous than any spider weaving her web, like a spell. These INFLUENCES are always inventing causes of hatred and revenge, marking you as their victim.

Will you struggle against these INFLUENCES with the unaided force of your own good intentions? Will you trample the poisonous jungle with bare feet? Conscious of your own honesty, will you meet the malicious, angry, revenging INFLUENCES, that know no mercy or scruple, without the only power which can overcome them?

Chapter Six - The Influence of the Beast

Once, when men were obsessed by a feeling within, like the spirit of a beast, whether wolf, snake, dog or pig, such an obsession was ascribed to "Satan" and his dark horde of devils.

"Satan" was the name given to that particular kind of demon which made man bestial, and for convenience we may still refer to that INFLUENCE as Satanic.

When our ancestors became obsessed with degrading thoughts, through no fault of their own, but by this terrible INFLUENCE, they felt that they had fallen into the power of Satan.

(a) Now, a dog may be, and frequently is, a respectable member of the animal kingdom. But a man, so possessed of this INFLUENCE, and so cast down from his estate as a man, that *he* is a dog, is a mongrel cur, unfit for the society of young people, full of foul nastiness. His spiritual manhood is attacked by this INFLUENCE, and if he succumbs, it will be lost; then his spiritual condition will be gradually made manifest in his body, and the work of the INFLUENCE will be complete.

It is not necessary to elaborate an unpleasant subject, except to say that this is the greatest disaster the ordinary mind can imagine. The mind despises that condition, with such a repulsion, that to be called a son of a dog, male or female, has always been felt the bitterest epithet possible.

Certainly to a man, no worse fate can be thought of, than to lose his manhood, spiritually, mentally, integrally, determinately or physically.

(b) This INFLUENCE is also felt by those who become imbued with a wolfish or snarling habit, or who meet such expressions in others. Lycanthropia still exists, more subtle and secret than ever, but still snarling and growling at us through those who are possessed with a lust to take from us all that we have and to even take the right to live at all.

(c) The INFLUENCE sometimes surrounds a girl or young woman, appearing to be felt by her as a "cattish" or feline force. Spiritually the cat is the symbol of spinsterhood. There are many places where this INFLUENCE is felt to such a degree that all the girls become "old maids," through no fault of their own, and in spite of having winsome and desirable characters. Sometimes a girl can break the spell by going away from that place, but usually the INFLUENCE pursues her and may so fasten on the heart as to make her cattish or oldmaidish in character. Then, even if the INFLUENCE can be overcome enough to permit of marriage, she remains an "old maid" in character, and such are called the worst kind.

(d) The mule is a symbol, not only of stubbornness, but also of sterility. Not every one feels this INFLUENCE as sterility, but over some its power is supreme. One who feels that life's object is lost if she has no child, is

sometimes so entangled by this INFLUENCE that her hope becomes hopeless and her desire turns to despair. Then, when life is void to her, the INFLUENCE whispers that it is her own fault, and that she is worthless and should commit suicide. Dear Sister, do not believe it. Satan was a liar from the beginning. All will be well when you are relieved from his power!

Again, when we find the world unaccountably stubborn around us, it is this INFLUENCE of the beast, injecting that mulish spirit, like poison, into the air.

(e) The loyalty of those we love or who smile upon us to our faces, could be forever depended upon in a world free of the treacherous INFLUENCE, symbolized by the snake. But that is not this world, as everyone knows. We were constituted for *that* world, more than for this one, or we would not again and again, believe and believe still again what people say to us — or that they are working in our interests, even after we find out by bitter experience, over and over, that we so make ourselves liable to disappointment.

Do not blame your friend who turns against you. He is possessed of this INFLUENCE and cannot help it. Nor can you, in your own strength, help him. Only the CHRISTPOWER can make him free, when he will be your own loving friend again. In such a case, as far only as his treachery toward you is concerned, you can accept the CHRISTPOWER for him, as we shall see on another page. The folk lores of many different races show that a snakish INFLUENCE has been almost universally felt, and primitive hymns voice the belief caused by that feeling, for instance:

> "Ol' Satan, he's a snake in the grass,
> "Yes, my Lord!"

This snake spirit is the most insidious form of this INFLUENCE. Entering into a husband or wife it disturbs the oneness of that relationship, by first diverging the thoughts, then creating aims in the breasts of each, which the other does not share, and finally creating a positive disloyalty, which, if not cast out, inevitably ends in a dissolution of the marriage, whether made physical by divorce or annulment, or not.

The INFLUENCES which come with bestial suggestions are many, and bring a man to the precipice, over which, if not saved, he will be thrust. There lie broken friendships, ruined lives, and blighted hopes!

(f) The spirit of swine, or the INFLUENCE of hoggishness is a terribly alive force in the world. You may feel that your work is good and useful, but you are surrounded by hogs who "swill everything."

Dear Brother, beware of this INFLUENCE, for it will deny you the right to exist. It will monopolize everything you should have. It will take away the benefit of all your opportunities and leave you in the mire. Call it by any name you will, Satan, the Beast, or the spirit of evil, its real existence as the INFLUENCE of hoggishness, cannot be denied. It does not hide insidiously, as other

INFLUENCES do, nor is it subtle as others are. It is terribly blatant — Satan sitting in the high places of the Earth — and actually boasting of his cloven hoof!

You are being openly and brazenly squeezed to death! Your own efforts can only feed the swine more, for you are not in a physical net, but a spiritual one. To be free, it is not more knowledge or more physical strength that you need, it is the CHRISTPOWER!

Nothing else can avail you but that power, and by the acceptance of that power you can be free!

(g) Idiocy and every kind of foolishness come from the beast INFLUENCE. If your child or any loved one seems to be dull of comprehension, or inconsequential, exciting the suggestion in others that he is a "goose" or "donkey" or that he is "asinine," do not blame or punish him. He is the greatest sufferer himself from the INFLUENCE which obsesses him. The goose is the symbol of silliness and the ass of foolish endeavors. Some are so contrarily foolish, that the more you try to teach them the less they learn. No use to provide tuition, books, rules and regulations for such; the INFLUENCE cannot be exorcised in that way.

(h) Corpulence is another phase of this INFLUENCE. But here a distinction must be drawn between that which is natural and beautiful and that which is unsightly and deforming. Natural plumpness, especially in children, cannot properly be called corpulence. Yet this INFLUENCE attacks the mind with its suggestion that the body has too much adipose tissue, even when, with-

out such an attack, the same degree of plumpness would not be considered excessive. Such an attack on the mind must be repulsed first, before the bodily condition can be improved, and without the CHRISTPOWER it is impossible to withstand and repulse that attack, and cast out the demon of corpulence.

There is a kingdom of bestial influences analogous to the ordinary, harmless, beautiful animal kingdom. But how different! Where a bird or quadruped is wonderful in its beauty or sagacity, the INFLUENCE. Selecting its own most degrading aspect, names it after that animal.

No wonder our fathers called this INFLUENCE by the worst name they could find — Satan.

Chapter Seven - The Influences Attacking Health

The Science of medicine, so called, has made wonderful strides in late years, and advanced from a stage where cathartics administered to, and blood taken from, the patient, comprised the whole prescription for every imaginable sickness or disease.

Scientists are gradually proving, to their own satisfaction, that certain diseases are caused by "germs," i.e., alive things, so small as to be invisible in the strongest microscope, which they judge must necessarily be present, for they can find no other "rational" explanation of the diseases that afflict mankind.

Whether the scientist calls the "disease," smallpox or scarlet-fever or measles or whooping cough or mumps or leprosy, the "germ" is his theory. No one has ever seen any "germs" of those diseases, they simply figure out that the influences felt must come from something alive, hence the theory of "germs."

It is true that in certain other diseases, such as malaria, tiny forms can be seen by the aid of a strong microscope. But the scientists claim that these forms are not the "germs" themselves, but "baccilli," that is, animals who are themselves afflicted with "germs."

For twenty years of history these unseen terrors have been called "germs," but for more than 4000 years prior to that time they have been called "demons." Whether our fathers were right in the word they used for 4000 years, or modern scientists are right in the word they have used for twenty years, is a matter of definition only. Our fathers felt the INFLUENCE of such things and called it by the name of the demon Meresin.

To them Meresin, with his multitude of evil spirits, was a reality, because the diseases caused by the so-called "germs" actually afflicted them. Let us not quarrel about the definition of a word, when we are confronted with a terrible reality, such as a disease or disability in ourselves or loved ones. You who feel that your affliction is caused by "Meresin," and you who attribute it to "earth spirits," and you who call it "malicious animal magnetism," and you who say it is but a "germ," all mean the same thing, namely, that INFLUENCE cast upon life, which causes the "claim" of pain and sickness. This being understood, we may, for the purpose of definition, call such INFLUENCE in general by the name of Meresin.

These Meresin influences come in many forms, which may be for our purpose divided into:

(a) *Fevers,* or INFLUENCES which seek to increase the usual rate at which the blood flows, and at which all the functions of the body proceed;

(b) Constipations and colds, or influences which retard the life of the body and diminish the normal action of life in any way;

(c) Congestions, or INFLUENCES disturbing the normal distribution through the body of its blood and its life, frequently combining a feverish influence in one part of the body, with a retarding influence in another.

(d) Pain; which is a separate INFLUENCE from all the others, though they all lead to conditions where this INFLUENCE can enter in.

(e) Depression of Spirits. Scientists say that if you have the "blues" your liver or some other organ is to blame. A "germ" has got into it, they say, which, although lodged for instance in the liver, affects the mind and brain. They are not able to explain why a "germ" can attack one place and thereby cause disturbance in a totally different place.

(f) Weakness. This INFLUENCE saps the vitality of some part, or of the whole man. Children's bad habits of every kind are mere weaknesses. The drink habit is a weakness. Deafness, eyestrain, etc., are weaknesses. It is not natural or normal to be weak in any particular. After countless years of development, man's body is naturally and normally perfect in its own strength, and but for the INFLUENCES, would never feel any weakness, so-called, or insufficiency of strength to meet and bravely face and overcome any and every condition. Our fathers classified this branch of the Meresin IN-

FLUENCE as Vampirish, because the weakness caused thereby resembles an actual loss of blood and of vitality.

Whatever theory may be urged by scientists, physicians or others, as to the intrinsic cause of pain, they all agree that the attitude of the patient's mind has at least something to do with it.

Some scientists claim that their medicines have certain effects only because it is the mental attitude of the world that such medicines actually have such effects. Others offer no explanation whatever, but still say that the medicine, to be most "effective," must be taken while the patient is in a cheerful and hopeful frame of mind.

So all agree that there is "mind-stuff" in disease and pain — even those who claim that there is "matter" or "material substance" therein. But all classes of scientists admit that they do not know the nature either of "mind-stuff" or of "matter," so the controversy is wholly academic.

We do not have to decide between, or pin our faith to either, of the contentions of the present day, as to the intrinsic nature of mind, matter, disease, pain or weakness. What the name or fundamental nature of the INFLUENCE may be, does not cause or prevent its power over us, nor invite it in nor drive it out. What we actually feel, need not be given this name or that name. It is there; we feel it to be alive; we know its power over us by actual experience and not by theory; and many know how helpless it is to struggle against it — without the CHRISTPOWER.

The most terrible visitation of this INFLUENCE is when it attacks childhood. It shocks the senses and ideals of the mind to see a child suffer. When a fond parent or sister has to stand by, unable to battle against the terrible INFLUENCE attacking the little one, it seems as if hope itself is going out, like as if darkness blotted out the sky at midday!

If a little one suffers, the one who loves it suffers too, and that one may, for the little one, accept the CHRISTPOWER.

(g) Childlessness is a kind of suffering from this INFLUENCE. It seems that in cases where body and brain are developed to the highest and noblest and strongest degree, where many INFLUENCES have been conquered and one would say, "Here is a perfect specimen," an influence of childlessness, the enemy of our race, creeps in, to make that high development of no effect for the future.

No man can satisfactorily explain to others why there should be, or how there came to be, such an INFLUENCE, that could be called the "enemy of our race."

As stated in Chapter One, materialists might say that there always was the same quantity of matter and nothing else, that this "matter" was first in the form of gas, then by "attraction" (and they cannot explain what they mean by that word) the gas became subject to the pressure of its own weight, and so became liquid, and finally solid. That the gas had a "will to exist in any form," and when it became liquid, it experienced an "advancement" and so developed another will, slightly at variance with the first will, namely, a "will to exist in advanced forms." These two wills, they say, have been at variance and fighting ever since — and because the "will to live in advanced form" is opposed to that part of the "will to exist in any form" which would perpetuate the life of what we call low, cruel, and base, and since there are many expressions of each will, it follows that certain expressions of the "will to live in any form, e. g., basely and bestially," seek occasion to attack that which would advance. Therefore, they may be termed enemies of our race.

This explanation does not go far enough to satisfy anybody, nor could it be possible for material scientists to formulate a theory that would, for the reason that the truth is only partly revealed to them and only partly explainable to man.

If the sacred secret in its entirety were reserved until man is ready to hear, it yet appears that the scientists recognize the INFLUENCES, but here call them "Expressions of the will to live in base forms."

This volume is not for the purpose of disputing terms or urging one word or name over another. Enough that all men recognize and feel the INFLUENCES, no matter what name they call them.

Chapter Eight - The Influences Causing Strife

Under this head we may properly consider wars between nations, litigation between individuals, bad temper, estrangements, misunderstandings of every kind.

It is evident that no two people would waste their time and substance in a fight of any kind, unless some feeling made their respective points of view divergent.

There are two ways in which points of view may be so radically divergent as to cause strife; *(a)* as to justice and right; *(b)* as to the expected result of the fight.

It is conceivable that two might fight for a prize, independent of any difference of opinion as to what was just and right. It is also conceivable that in the face of certain defeat one might fight for what he believed to be just and right.

But nearly all fights result from the double obsession, i.e., each side is obsessed with the idea that he is in the right, and also obsessed with the idea that the result of the fight will be an advantage to him.

These feelings, or obsessions, are caused by some INFLUENCES which seem to delight in stirring up strife. Our fathers called these influences "Abaddon." They recognized the cruel power of such, and many writers have declared wars to be brought about by fate, so powerful did they deem these INFLUENCES to be.

Never, before the application of the CHRISTPOWER, have any of these INFLUENCES, or strife demons, been conquered. They work in sets, frequently putting brother against brother, parent against child, and even husband against wife.

It is easy to recognize the strife obsession, especially in another. Antagonism is so contrary to the ordinary dictates of the human heart that its appearance toward yourself is a shock hard to bear. Yet the person so obsessed is more to be pitied than blamed. Ordinarily, the human heart would be kind and loving. Obsessed with this INFLUENCE, it becomes a foe instead of a friend.

Chapter Nine - The Influence Causing Self-accusation

Seventh on the list of INFLUENCES, classified in olden days, was the troop of "demons who drove men to despair" by entering into the heart and infusing therein a false spirit of self-accusation, self-depreciation, self-centered hopelessness, remorse for real or fancied mistakes and grovelling failure.

While few are entirely free from this INFLUENCE, a great many do not feel its power to the verge of despair, and are able, in their own strength, to disregard it for a season.

But to some, this DIABOLIS INFLUENCE, as we may call it, is so real and oppressive that they feel they will be driven to suicide, if relief does not come.

No one, who has not felt it, can understand the real pain of the so-called "blues."

This INFLUENCE may, as yet, only have a slight hold on you, and you may only have a slight attack of despondency. Its usual way is to visit but gently at first, gradually increasing in violence, bringing on at last hysterical fits of accelerating intensity.

When oppressed by this INFLUENCE, the world seems black, your best beloved seems disloyal and you seem to be sinking down into the depths of woe.

Then it leaves you for a while, but soon returns, often seeming to return exactly with the moon's phases — thus, if it is a full moon when the "blues" take you, look out for the next full moon. And at whatever phase of the moon you are attacked, look out for the same thing at the same phase of the moon.

Scientists have tried to discover why this INFLUENCE should seem to be affected by the moon, and have failed to establish any scientific connection between despondency and the moon. They say that the fact that the phases of the moon were important in ancient witchcraft, and the fact that the moon seems even to make dogs howl, must remain forever unexplained.

However that may be, and whether or not the INFLUENCES of despondency even know that there is a moon, the fact remains, as anyone can observe for himself, by keeping a diary of other people's "blues," that they often return, however slightly, with the exact regularity of the moon.

This INFLUENCE is a reality of such threatening aspect, that the proudest and strongest may well fear it. An enemy who does not storm the citadel from without, is the more to be feared. An insidious, sneaking enemy, who enters the very heart of you, and pretends to be you, with the lie that it is you, — you accusing yourself — this INFLUENCE cannot be thrown out or cast down by your own strength.

It turns your mind inward upon habits or weaknesses or undeveloped spots, and broods upon them, accusing you of human weaknesses as though they were the grossest of crimes.

Black as the hell-cat it is, it assumes the robe of an angel of light, and tortures the soul by pretending to be that sacred monitor. Conscience, "deceiving even the elect!"

Chapter Ten - Mammon

One's own experience teaches that there is some subtle INFLUENCE about money.

It is not the money itself which is the root of evil but a strange and almost uncanny feeling about it, which enters into the nature of a man, transforming him from being the center and source of all supply, into a clutching miser.

Strange as it may seem until we give the matter real thought, it is not the rich of this world who are the victims of this INFLUENCE. They who do not want for money are free from this INFLUENCE, and they who do want, are oppressed by it.

This is not to say that the rich are better than the would-be-rich. Far from it; other terrible INFLUENCES oppress them; but it is certain that they are better off as regards this particular INFLUENCE. They who do not want for money are free from the demon Mammon.

This message cannot come to one not ready to receive it. Such an one may have this INFLUENCE seated in his high will. This demon does not attract gold to its victims, because of its nature, as more particularly referred to elsewhere. This INFLUENCE keeps gold away, yet clings so convulsively to what gold one has, as to prevent any acceptance of the CHRISTPOWER by giving it up.

If such an one has read thus far, he has, from his point of view, been done a great injury by this message. For it is inevitable that he must choose either to pamper the INFLUENCE — Mammon — or to accept the CHRISTPOWER; if he cannot or will not do the latter, it is certain that the influence will set itself against him, and will inevitably banish from that man the gold itself — and never shall he have his heart's desire as long as gold is his God!

Those who make sacrifice of the false god, who humbly come to the CHRISTPOWER and accept, can be placed on a new and different basis as to money — a basis different from any they have ever before experienced.

Yes! By that wonderful CHRISTPOWER, I say in all humility and reverence, the influence which makes the "will-o'-the-wisp," teasing, calling, yet vanishing, effect, ever luring but never realizable, can be forever banished. This INFLUENCE desires to be worshipped much in little gold — ye who are subject the most to this baneful INFLUENCE, have the least, but will find it the hardest to accept and sacrifice; yet if ye do accept, the CHRISTPOWER can make you free!

To realize what freedom from the spirit of Mammon means, is to realize the most radical reversal of former standards. One who has hitherto, by reason of that INFLUENCE, always failed to get "enough money" and has had to be close and economical at the best of times, suddenly finds himself, as it were, at the center of all supply.

This INFLUENCE is the curse of poverty and want, the "wolf at the door." This is he who drives men from "hand to mouth," ever keeping them under, and dependent upon circumstances. This is not gold, but the want of it; the demon who dangles the gold in front of your eyes, drawing it ever backward to lure you into the abyss.

Chapter Eleven - Sorrow and Disappointment

As we examine nature, observing the so-called lower forms, and so "upward," in the scale of development, we see that there is a point where even some animals become more affected by sorrow and disappointment than by pain.

Without praising any animal, or suggesting a usefulness, which it does not exhibit, there yet must be conceded to be well authenticated instances where horses and dogs have grieved to death over the loss of their two-footed masters.

So man, highly organized, of sensitive and finely-poised nature, early discovered that he could be more severely affected by sorrow and disappointment, than by the most excruciating physical agony.

Waves and waves of sorrow have passed over the race long, long ago. This was one of the first of the INFLUENCES to be felt, and men tried to propitiate it by setting up its image as a god, to whom children were sacrificed by being burnt alive.

Moloch, the name of horror, was the name given the Prince of the sorrow demons.

That this INFLUENCE is very much alive to-day no one will deny. Call it what you will, the fact remains that the heart is attacked by INFLUENCES as much as the body.

Impending misfortune vanishes when this INFLU-ENCE is cast out.

This INFLUENCE brings all sorts of calamity upon you; it bereaves you, it disappoints you at every turn. Everything may be going smoothly, hopes for the future springing high in your breast, those you love a constant joy, and no cloud in sight, when suddenly the blow falls.

Man in his arrogance, sometimes thinks he is the whole universe, and that no spirits exist except himself. Serene in that confidence, he anticipates no disaster, but takes his mental ease, never dreaming of the insidi-ous foe. Not warned by past experiences of trouble and sorrow coming suddenly, he is all unprepared to meet the disaster.

Bereaved, or smitten with vital physical infirmity, or arrested and cast into prison, or despoiled of all, or cheated by trusted friend, like lightning out of a clear sky, this INFLUENCE attacks you.

There are men who are kept alive by their hopes and ambitions. In the hour of disappointment these die of a broken heart or commit suicide.

This INFLUENCE, pretending to lead men into light, brings them into the darkness of despair. The heavens seem closed to prayers. Such men are hedged in by bit-terness, as with heavy chains. They become disor-ganized, do not seem themselves, seem as if pulled in pieces.

When attacked by this INFLUENCE, men wish they had never been born, and crave for death to relieve their misery. Then one says with Job:

11. Why died I not,...

13. For now should I have lain still and been quiet, I should have slept: then had I been at rest.

17. There the wicked cease from troubling; and there the weary be at rest.

20. Wherefore is light given to him that is in misery, and life unto the bitter in soul;

21. Which long for death, but it cometh not;

25. For the thing which I greatly feared is come upon me;

26. I was not in safety, neither had I rest, neither was I quiet; yet trouble came.— Job III: 11, 13, 17, 20, 21, 25, 26.

The height of joy and perfect freedom are so far removed from sorrow and despair, that though I point earnestly and knowingly to that Height, one in the depth cannot perfectly receive the message.

To cast out of your life such an INFLUENCE, is more than to save your physical life — to save only that life would be no benefit to one who longed for death, — it is to place your feet on the mountain!

Chapter Twelve - Injustice

Those who have been thus far sheltered from the world, and not attacked by the INFLUENCE in this chapter referred to, can have no conception or understanding of the feelings of those who are the victims of injustice.

The terrors willingly braved, for the sake of justice, by the heroes of history, are unreal to those who have not experienced injustice.

Yet in each there is, deep down, such a resistance to injustice, that if he does become its victim, a new side to his character appears, and all his desires merge into one, — that he have justice!

Our fathers recognized that injustice comes from an INFLUENCE, which to them was so mysterious that they named it Lucifer, and, as Justice was conceived by them to be the highest deity, or attribute of deity, so the origin of injustice was typified by the fall from heaven of its brightest angel. They further had it that when Lucifer and his angels of injustice were vanquished in heaven, they were thrown onto the Earth, there to practice their wicked INFLUENCE upon the affairs of men, and have power for a season. That season was to last until the CHRISTPOWER should prevail.

We do not have to subscribe to any of the words used by those men of olden time, to know that the INFLUENCE of injustice is rampant to-day, as of yore.

We see it and experience it every day. Even courts can not always do justice. The most honest judge is often swayed by prejudice, which is easily created by clever attorneys.

Certain wrongs can never be righted by appealing to the courts, and in many cases the triumph of justice is only in name.

The recognition that injustice is an INFLUENCE, has overcome it, in hundreds of cases, — where the very courts of our land were asked to bolster up unjust causes. In many of those cases the courts had already given unjust decisions, and appeals had been taken, before the INFLUENCES causing such injustice had been cast out.

Many other kinds of injustice are rampant in the world to-day. Brother is unjust to brother, sister to sister, your best-beloved to you, and, in fact, this INFLUENCE — Lucifer — is so persistent and so malignant that it attacks nearly everybody, some more, some less.

If you are attacked by this INFLUENCE, the sign of it will be that you feel yourself to be unjustly treated.

Nothing can save you from it but the CHRISTPOWER. You may try to fight against it in your own strength, but so you will only change it and not abate it. Without the CHRISTPOWER, man's strength is not able to cope with this INFLUENCE. You will remember that our ancestors held that there was a great battle in heaven, between Justice and Lucifer, before Lucifer could be cast out. How could a man then, in his own strength, hope to conquer it?

Chapter Thirteen – Bad Luck

Twelfth on the ancient lists of kinds of demons were the demons of bad luck — spirits causing man to just miss good fortune of all kinds and entangling him in a network of adverse circumstances.

A man has just ten minutes to catch a train and the station is five minutes' ride on the street cars. Although at all times when it is not important to him he sees those street cars go by every two minutes, this time he has to wait eight minutes and so loses his train — "bad luck."

Another just happens to be walking under the edge of a building, when a brick gets dislodged and hits him on the head — "bad luck."

Another walks under ladders again and again with his old clothes on and nothing happens. But the day he has on a new suit, a pail of paint falls off the ladder and splashes him — "bad luck."

Soldiers shoot rifles with steady aim at the enemy, but only kill about one for each three hundred shots. A boy playing with an old pistol, which he does not know is loaded, will, if he accidentally discharges it, kill his playmate nearly every time. Why? "Bad luck."

Why does bread always fall on the carpet buttered side down?

Why do the stocks you happen to buy always go down instead of up?

Why do you always find you have lent money to people who will not or can not repay, while if you borrow money yourself you have to repay?

Where does the "jinx" come from that seems so ready to crush all enterprise?

Who dares to say he is free from every pain, trouble, and misfortune, unless he, at the same time "knocks on wood" to keep away the jinx of bad luck?

Only to ask these questions brings it home to us that there certainly is a very real INFLUENCE interfering in human affairs.

This INFLUENCE often assumes the disguise of some of the other INFLUENCES and therefore the greatest care is necessary in telling me about it so that I may know certainly which INFLUENCE it is which is destroying you.

You may be the victim of false gods or deceptive ideals and yet think you are attacked by the "bad luck" INFLUENCE.

Or the "bad luck" INFLUENCE may be attacking you in such a subtle way as to make you think you are the victim of Beelzebub.

Again you may feel that the spirit of slander is abroad against you — that Apollyon has you in his foul grip — when in reality it is the bad luck INFLUENCE surrounding you with accidental misconstructions of words perhaps well intentioned.

Or, accidents brought about by this INFLUENCE, may seem to be deliberate mischiefs, creating real anger — apparently the work of the Belial INFLUENCE.

You may fear revenge, and your fear may be wholly created by some mischance brought about by the Antichrist INFLUENCE - thus does Antichrist ape Asmodeus.

In one sense there is no such thing as an accident. Every mischance is the wilful work of the Antichrist INFLUENCE. So that a stronger force than you are (in your own strength) deliberately causes against you those so-called accidents and failures of luck. Now, there is a sense in which something deliberately caused by a stronger power cannot be said to be an accident.

This INFLUENCE Constantly deceives its victims with the suggestion that their "hick will turn" — holding out false hopes. No one has ever known any "law of chances" to work out in real life, yet this INFLUENCE Constantly beguiles men into believing that there is such a thing as a "law of chances," by which the luck must turn.

But if you will relax your preconceived ideas on this point you must perceive that as long as you are the victim of the INFLUENCE your "luck will never turn"; whenever it is not one thing it will be another, until at last you accept the CHRISTPOWER, and the bad luck INFLUENCE is cast out of your life.

Oh, what a difference in one's life when Antichrist is cast out!

Chapter Fourteen - Astarte the Goddess

There is an influence abroad in the world which plays upon the nerve centers of man — as if an unseen hand were to reach down into a telephone switchboard and disturb the connections.

Delicately poised, if let alone, the intricate machinery of the nerve center works smoothly and harmoniously, perfectly connecting the will with the act, the ideal with the conduct and the thought with the speech.

When the hand of the INFLUENCE pulls out a plug or disconnects a wire, of man's perfect mechanism, it seems as if he were doing it himself, so terribly near this INFLUENCE seems. And indeed, when he dreams, and this INFLUENCE robs him of the connection between nerve and imagery, so near it is, that he will swear that it is he, himself, and will hardly at all believe that it is the oldest known of all the INFLUENCES that is victimizing him.

In the earliest dawn of history Astarte or Astoreth was the name given to the INFLUENCE that was conceived of as the queen of hell; also called "Babylon." This INFLUENCE was at all times felt as a disconnecting force. A man would stand speechless at the very moment when he would have given his life to be able to say the right thing — or would not be able to move his hand at the instant when such movement was vital — or would lose control over any part of himself — then he would say he was afflicted of Astarte.

To-day this INFLUENCE is stronger than ever before, and while we know better now than to call it a goddess, it is certainly just as real as if it actually had the sex and majesty of one. And with what goddess beauty it can fraudulently clothe its foul visions, and with what silvery voices it can call men to destruction!

There is no defense against this INFLUENCE except the CHRISTPOWER. Purity, prayer, fasting, or high resolves are all useless, because this INFLUENCE disturbs the connection between your purity, prayer, fasting and high resolves on the one hand, and your nerves on the other.

Purity is good for its own sake, but it is not a defense against this INFLUENCE. Prayer and fasting and high resolves have carried men past many a dangerous milestone, but not past this one.

Young and old are victimized and often goaded into suicide by this terribly distracting, disconnecting and disturbing INFLUENCE. The brightest and bravest men and women, in the flower of their youth and strength, are perverted, disconnected, distracted and driven into madness, despair and suicide by this INFLUENCE. It comes first in dreams, in which the victim sees himself perhaps the helpless victim of a vampire or the raging pursuer of a helpless one. One, who, in waking hours, is the mildest and gentlest of men, will see himself committing a foul crime — perhaps murder — and on awakening will feel a sense of guilt. But he is not at fault or to blame. There is not necessarily any evil in him that he should have such a dream. It is the INFLUENCE.

Do not, my brother, my sister, believe that you are responsible, morally, for your dreams, or feel that there is any foul spot in you because you have foul dreams. You have no more to do with it than the battery has to do with the bell after the wire is cut. All that is the matter is that the Astarte INFLUENCE has commenced an attack upon you. Though I say, that is all, it is surely terrible enough. For this INFLUENCE never leaves its victim except for a season. It will leave you, it will return and still return, again and again, oftener and oftener, until it has you completely in its power.

Chapter Fifteen - Thirteen Adverse Spirits

The thirteen kinds of INFLUENCES adverse to the human race have many variations; or, as our ancestors felt those INFLUENCES, it would be more correct to say that each prince of darkness has many and differing imps in his train.

Some people now call them "earth spirits," because they attack us here and now, on this earth, and because they do not inhabit some far distant hell, but work to make hell on earth.

All primitive peoples feel the INFLUENCES and call them demons. Natives of the farthest distant lands have similar rites and similar beliefs about demons. For instance in Tibet, and in West Africa, and in Siam, and among the North Dakota Indians, the art of conjuring into puppets the "demons" is a recognized rite.

The latest investigations of travelers to every primitive tribe in the world have been gathered together by Frazer and Ernest Crawley in their respective books, "Golden Bough," and the "Mystic Rose." To these facts they have added reports of old customs in various counties in England, Germany, France and Russia. As might be expected, the same INFLUENCES are felt everywhere, though called by different names in different places. The "Mystic Rose" is especially instructive.

The fear of evil spirits enters into the marriage ceremonies of the South Celebes.

The sedan chair in which a Manchu bride goes to the house of the bridegroom, is disinfected with incense to keep away evil spirits.

In Russia all doors and windows are closed at a wedding to keep out the INFLUENCE of childlessness.

Pontianak is the name given the INFLUENCE against childbirth by the natives of Amboina and Ceram.

Maoris identify the flowing of blood with the evil spirit Kahnkahn.

Among the Sonthals, evil spirits are everywhere.

In Egypt the Ginn pervade everything.

Karlits feel the INFLUENCES of spirits of the air.

New Caledonians feel the INFLUENCES of sickness and death and call them spirits.

In Siam, spirits are thought to swarm in the air.

The Kurnai live a life of dread of spells.

Natives of Hatam dread poison infused in atmosphere.

It is always the Spiritual danger which makes a man "taboo," and it is dangerous to others as soon as it descends upon him, and fills him with visno or electric force.

Then "he is able both to cause and cure, disease, rain, wind, thunder, and hail."

Amongst the Dieri and other tribes of South Australia, disease is universally felt to come from devils — Cootchie.

Cambodians believe the Arak are spirits of disease.

Crawley adds that in primitive belief devils were created by man in this wise — the picture of a hated enemy on the brain — when he shuts his eyes the image appears — the man's soul acquires "an image of his foe, a tiny but evil spirit which appears within him, he knows not how or whence." INFLUENCES so work through human agencies — vetches.

Amongst the Bongos, old women are especially suspected of alliance with wicked spirits.

In British Guiana, the destroying spirit, "Kanaima," possesses the man and then he is called the Kanaima.

Among the Mandingoes he is called "Mumbo Jumbo."

In East Central Africa the people give an offering of flour to the spirits when a person is ill. The spirits regale them of the flour. In Halmahera also, they believe the spirits eat the essence of food.

The Hill Dyaks place choice morsels where the spirits can eat their essence. Amongst the Yorubas, evil spirits are supposed to cause the illnesses of children.

The spirits are supposed to eat the spiritual part of the children's food.

Central Australians say a magic evil influence, called Arungquiltha, causes all contagion.

Badi is the name given by the Malays to the evil influence pursuing everything that has life, it brings illness of every conceivable kind.

Laplanders attribute disease to magic birds.

People of the Kei Islands, Australian Islanders, East Central Africans, as well as the Dakota Indians, suck the injured part or apply the cupping process to draw out the evil spirit.

"This," remarks Crawley, "is scientific in a way," (Mystic Rose, p. 86).

All these learned writers make their own so-called science harmonize with the so-called superstition of the primitive peoples of the whole world.

Australian women "sing," e. g., "I love you," and "May your spirit be brave and true," over food giving it a hoemeopathical magical quality, so that when eaten by the man, he receives the blessings so intended.

"Not only civilized ideas," adds Crawley, "but human systems and institutions of the most important character are built on these foundations."

Bulgarians before drinking make the sign of the cross, to prevent the devil entering the body with the liquor.

Fasting was — similarly — to prevent evil spirits from entering the body.

In the Aroo Islands, Kola Kobroor, the Babar Islands, Islands of Wetar, Java, Nias, Amboina, Uliase and Bum, they believe in evil spirits that particularly oppress women.

The Battas attribute anger to evil spirits.

When a man is sick, to drive away the evil spirits, the Aru Islanders fire off guns round the house, the Ceramese, Watubela and Kei Island natives move the sick man secretly to another house to "deceive the spirits." In Celebes a dummy is left in the sick man's bed.

A mourner in Andaman Islands will shoot arrows into the jungle thinking that he hits evil spirits.

A wide generalization can be made of all the experiences felt by mankind, and Crawley, speaking as a scientist, referring to the INFLUENCES, says that such a wide generalization (i.e., that all men feel the spirit INFLUENCES), "has within it, though concealed in fallacy, a scientific truth, destined to emerge after a training in analysis." (Page 199).

Dyaks attribute disease and death to INFLUENCES called by them "Petara."

The Mintra of the Malay Peninsula feel a separate IN-FLUENCE, differing and separately named, corresponding to every disease known to them.

The Tasmanian attributes every gnawing pain to the presence within him of an INFLUENCE which had formerly possessed some man now dead.

Zulus sacrifice cattle (and thus accept the freedom from INFLUENCES). In all parts of the world the sacrifice of objects or animals is made.

Suppose all tribes of men sprung or developed from separate causes in places far different from each other. Then suppose you visited each tribe on a fine day but found them all in possession of umbrellas. The conclusion would be irresistible that in each of those places rain sometimes fell.

So, when the same idea of sacrifice, to ward off evil spirits, is found in every corner of the earth, the logician argues therefrom that in each of those places such IN-FLUENCES actually exist.

There is a period in the growth when a sensitive feeling recognizes INFLUENCES not felt by thicker skins. Those men whose hearts have been large, have in all ages testified and do now testify, to the terrible presence of these adverse INFLUENCES.

Emanuel Swedenborg testified as follows:

"What wickedness there is in infernal spirits, may be manifest from their atrocious arts, which are so numerous that to enumerate them would fill a volume, and to describe them, many volumes; those arts are mostly unknown in the world. One kind relates to the abuses of correspondences; a second, to the abuses of the ultimates of Divine order; a third, to communication and influx of thoughts and affections, by conversions, by inspections, and by other spirits besides themselves, and by those sent from themselves; a fourth, to operations by phantasies; a fifth, to projections out of themselves, and consequent presence elsewhere than where they are with the body; a sixth, to pretenses, persuasions, and lies. By these arts they torment. But since all of these arts, except those which are effected by pretenses, persuasions, and lies are unknown in the world, I will not here describe them specifically, as well because they would not be comprehended, as because they are too bad to be told." [1]

All the thirteen black princes, as they were called, have troops of "black angels," or as we would call them, INFLUENCES.

Some fasten on the soul and present you in a bad light to others. They also set all others against you, against your plans and desires, and against your happiness; making you despised and hated without cause and making those who would otherwise gladly do your will and bless you in their hearts, plot against you.

Other INFLUENCES often oppress you by fits of despondency, melancholy, regret and remorse. You find yourself burdened by a sense of sin which something urges you to tell or by a passionate regret that you did something the way you did. Nothing but the

CHRISTPOWER can set you free, — free not only from the haunting fear of blame, not only from the INFLUENCE urging you forward to the precipice of self-accusation, but free in the knowledge that the past is forgotten, and the INFLUENCE which remembered it, is cast out and dead. Then at last you will feel safe that nothing can ever be remembered against you.

Other INFLUENCES attack the nerves. Should you sense pain without visible physical cause, you are being attacked by this INFLUENCE. Pain is of two kinds; of visible and invisible origin. For instance, if you cut yourself, the pain is of visible origin; on the other hand if you have pain first in one side of the face and then in the other, that is of invisible origin. These INFLUENCES fasten themselves upon the body and torment it unceasingly, and yet it can be endured by the soul without the madness that other INFLUENCES bring on.

The INFLUENCE that whispers and mutters in your brain gives you the sensations of hearing voices, dreaming dreams, seeing visions, etc. At first harmless, afterwards the most enervating. If you awake in the morning unrefreshed, feeling as if your lifeblood had been drained away, you are in the power of the vampire INFLUENCE draining your very soul.

There is also the "failure INFLUENCE." Man is the image and likeness of God, and is not doomed forever to fail. To accept the CHRISTPOWER for the casting out of the failure INFLUENCE evidences the highest degree of faith. But for that influence in your life you would hold all the threads of your fate in your own hands. Then when free from that INFLUENCE you will learn SUCCESS. No man can teach you success while you remain bound by the Spirit of Failure, but after you have accepted the CHRISTPOWER and become free from that INFLUENCE you will develop accordingly.

Another INFLUENCE brings on disease, either of yourself, or of some one dear to you, usually a child. Only the CHRISTPOWER can cast out this INFLUENCE. But it is given unto many to minister beneficially to disease. So until the CHRISTPOWER is accepted effectually for this INFLUENCE, fear not to use all so-called "material" means and advice from wise physicians, for none of these can prevent the effectiveness of accepting the CHRISTPOWER, and the eventual complete freedom from that INFLUENCE in your life.

The INFLUENCES, or "Earth Spirits," which come to individuals with the acquisition of anything which is believed to be valuable are very potent. Many cases might be recounted where a so-called curse rested upon the owner of some special diamond, ruby, or other stone. The like INFLUENCES come to those who have, or suddenly appreciate that they have, or who receive or win, any considerable money.

This INFLUENCE not only affects the mind and body, but is so sensitive and suspicious that, should you see One with His hand beckoning away from that money, it would whisper to your mind to guard the money closer and to beware of giving it up, "for," saith the INFLU-

ENCE, "he who offers help is insincere and only wants your money."

There are other INFLUENCES, such as the liquor and drug habits and many others, which oppress the soul of man. Many of these can be fought for a time with your own strength, and they can be conquered by some. But for any INFLUENCE whatever, the only sure relief is to be found in the CHRISTPOWER.

[1] "Heaven and the world of Spirits." Sec. 580.